Are You Ready for a
BACKPACK ADVENTURE?

Nature is all around you! And there is no better way to feel connected to nature than by taking a walk. The most important thing to take with you is curiosity, but you might want to gather up the items below in case you need them. Then hit the trail and explore!

THINGS TO BRING IN YOUR BACKPACK

This book & magnifying glass

Pen or pencil

Camera

Sunscreen

First aid kit

An extra layer of clothing

Bug spray

Snacks & water

Trail map & compass

NATURE PATCH STICKERS

There are 12 patch stickers in the back of the book that match **I SEE IT!** circles on some of the pages. When you find something in nature that matches something on an **I SEE IT!** page, put the sticker on the matching circle. See if you can collect them all!

I SEE IT!

PUT YOUR PATCH HERE

Squirrels

LOOK FOR THESE BUSHY-TAILED MAMMALS munching nuts and seeds in trees, or dashing across logs on the trail. A squirrel can leap 10 times its own length!

TRAIL TIPS

Here are some ways to have more fun wherever you walk!

BE PREPARED: bring water, snacks, and a first aid kit, and read the rules of the trail before you start your walk.

WALK AND TALK QUIETLY — you're more likely to see animals that way! But don't try to pet or feed wildlife.

TAKE YOUR TIME so you don't miss what's happening around you.

USE YOUR SENSES to see, hear, smell, and touch.

Take only pictures. Leave only footprints.

SMILE AND SAY HELLO to other hikers on the trail.

LEAVE YOUR NATURE FINDS for others to see, but take all your trash with you.

Leaves

LEAVES COME IN ALL SHAPES, SIZES, AND TEXTURES. Look for plant and tree leaves along the trail. Notice how their edges are different — some have smooth edges and others have pointy edges. Notice how leaves come in lots of different shades of green.

Plants use their leaves to turn sunlight into food!

What kinds of **LEAVES** do you see?

Maple

Aspen

Oak

Did you find any round, heart-shaped, or spear-shaped leaves?

Plantain

Ash

Horse chestnut

Don't touch this one — it stings!

Nettle

Find leaves with wavy, jagged, and smooth edges!

Clover

Fern

Dandelion

Take a LOOK

Look closely at the different parts of a leaf, such as the veins and the stem. Have any insects nibbled on the leaf?

TREES ON THE TRAIL

Spot differences between deciduous and evergreen trees!

Look at all the trees around you. Notice the differences in their shapes and in their leaves and needles. There are two kinds of trees: deciduous and evergreen.

DECIDUOUS TREES (dih-SID-juh-wus)

Oaks, maples, and other deciduous trees lose their leaves in the fall. Before they drop, the leaves change color from green to bright yellow, orange, or red! Deciduous trees are usually round at the top.

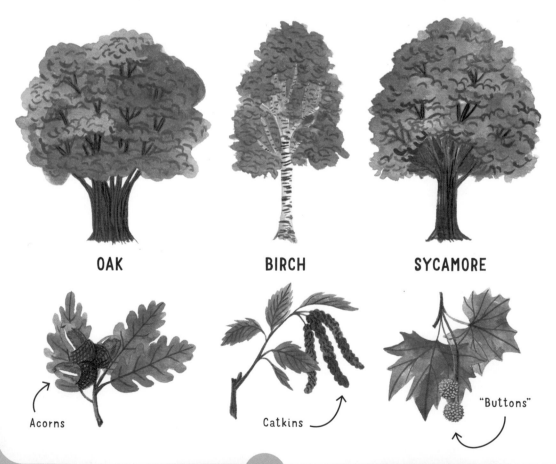

OAK   BIRCH   SYCAMORE

Acorns   Catkins   "Buttons"

EVERGREEN TREES

Some trees have needles instead of leaves. Instead of falling off all at once, needles cover the tree all year, which is why they are called "evergreens." Most trees like this are narrow and pointy at the top.

Many evergreens have cones made of small scales that hold the tree's seeds. When the scales open, the seeds fall to the ground.

The cones of a Coulter pine are bigger than a person's head!

FIR

PINE

SPRUCE

Fir needles are rounded and soft to touch.

Some pine trees have needles over a foot long!

Spruce needles are square and spiky.

Take a LOOK

Use your magnifying glass to look closely at the texture of tree bark. Do you see any sap, bugs, or tiny holes?

Birds

ALTHOUGH THEY COME IN MANY COLORS AND SHAPES, all birds have feathers and lay eggs. Birds don't have teeth; they use their strong beaks to eat food.

Every type of bird sings its own special song to attract or scare off other birds. How many different songs can you hear?

Blue jay

Most birds have fragile, hollow bones that make their bodies light enough to fly.

What kinds of **BIRDS** do you see?

Crow

Can you find a bird soaring in the sky?

Red-tailed hawk

Do you see any birds foraging for seeds, insects, or nectar?

Chickadee

Ruby-throated hummingbird

Robin

Mourning dove

Goldfinch

Can you spot a nest among the tree branches?

Cardinal

White-throated sparrow

Mallard

Take a LOOK

Find a feather? Look closely at the color and shape. What bird do you think it came from?

MUSIC on the Trail

Nature is full of materials you can use to make simple musical instruments! Try some of these ideas or come up with others depending on what you find.

ACORN CAP WHISTLE: Hold an acorn cap with your thumb knuckles touching, as shown. Your thumbs should form the letter V. Hold tight and blow hard between your thumbs to whistle. It takes practice, so keep trying. Adjust your thumbs or change the shape of the V until the whistle blows!

Create a V with your thumb knuckles touching.

STICK DRUM SET: Find a couple of sticks and bang them together or against a hollow log or tree stump. Create a simple rhythm pattern and have a partner repeat it.

STONES & SEEDS RATTLES: Bring small plastic containers on your hike and fill them with small stones, seeds, or acorns. Shake them around to hear what different sounds you can make.

MARCHING BAND. Join your friends and play your nature instruments on the trail together!

Insects

INSECTS HAVE SIX LEGS. Instead of bones, they have a hard shell called an exoskeleton (EK-soh-skel-uh-tun) that protects them. They help the earth by recycling dead materials, pollinating flowers, and providing food for many animals.

From ants and crickets on the ground, to bees and dragonflies in the air, insects are all around you.

Ladybug

There are more insects on earth than all other animals put together – including humans!

What kinds of **INSECTS** do you see?

Firefly

Beetle

Fly

Count how many flying insects you see on your walk.

Honeybee

Dragonfly

Mosquito

Do you hear any insects buzzing, chirping, hopping, or scratching?

Grasshopper

Cricket

Ant

Take a LOOK

Study the different parts of an insect, such as the wings, antennae, legs, head, and body.

WHAT'S IN THE SKY?

On your nature walk don't forget to look up! The sky is always above you. What color is the sky? Is the sun shining? (Just don't look directly at the sun — you could hurt your eyes.) Do you see clouds? Can you spot the moon, even though it's daytime?

SUN RAYS

Sometimes when the sun is blocked by clouds, you can see rays of light shining through.

RAINBOWS
It's always exciting to see a rainbow arching across the sky after it rains.

BIRDS
In the spring and fall, look for flocks of ducks and geese migrating north or south.

CLOUD GAZING

All clouds are made of masses of teeny-tiny water droplets or ice crystals. Different kinds of clouds have different names. Here are three of the most common. What kinds of clouds can you spot on your walk?

THIN & WISPY
CIRRUS (SYR-us)

These wispy clouds float high in the sky. They mean the weather may be changing soon.

FLUFFY & WHITE
CUMULUS (KYOOM-yuh-lus)

Big puffy white clouds in a blue sky mean good weather, but if they turn gray, rain may be coming.

SOLID GRAY
STRATUS
(STRA-tus)

A solid gray blanket of clouds usually means rain or snow is on the way.

Squirrels

LOOK FOR THESE BUSHY-TAILED MAMMALS munching nuts and seeds in trees, or dashing across logs on the trail. A squirrel can leap 10 times its own length!

Like all rodents, squirrels have teeth that never stop growing!

There are more than 280 species of squirrel in the world. The gray squirrel is the most common in North America. You may see the smaller red squirrel, too.

Gray squirrel

What other **SMALL MAMMALS** do you see?

Chipmunk

Do you hear a chipmunk or squirrel chattering?

Red squirrel

Cottontail rabbits

Can you find a squirrel's nest?

Keep your eyes out for bunnies nibbling on green leaves and grass!

Field mouse

Take a LOOK

Look under trees or on fallen logs for small piles of leftover seeds and shells where a squirrel ate a snack.

LISTEN UP!

Close your eyes for a few moments and listen to the sounds around you. Do you hear any of these things?

☐ A bird chirping

☐ Wind in the trees

☐ Rushing water

☐ Chipmunk chatter

☐ Rustling noises

☐ An insect buzzing

What else do you hear?

_____

_____

ANIMAL COPYCAT

Play follow-the-leader and learn how animals move!

Keep your eyes out for animals big and small.
If you spot one, notice how it moves.

Birds flap their wings, caterpillars inch along, and squirrels run and leap.

Take turns with a friend being the **LEADER** and the **FOLLOWER**. The leader moves like an animal and the follower copies the movement!

CAN YOU...

HOP like a frog?

DIG like a mole?

FLUTTER like
a butterfly?

SLITHER like a snake?

I SEE IT!

PUT YOUR
PATCH HERE

Worms

EARTHWORMS LIVE UNDERGROUND.
Their long, skinny bodies are made of
ringlike segments that help them tunnel
through the dirt. Worms eat a lot of dirt
and dead leaves. In fact, they eat half
their body weight each day!

Earthworms
breathe through
their skin!

To find a worm, try
digging through
damp soil or looking
on the sidewalk
after it rains.

Common
earthworm

What other kinds of **CREATURES** do you see?

Kneel down on the ground to see what you can find.

Ground snail

Beetle larvae

Ant with egg

Wood louse

Centipedes and millipedes have many legs, but snails and slugs have none!

Millipede

Centipede

Earwig

If you see a slug or snail, look for its trail of slime!

Slug

Take a LOOK

Look for tiny eggs and larvae hidden under rocks and logs. Those pale, wiggly larvae eventually grow into adult insects!

Nature CRITTERS

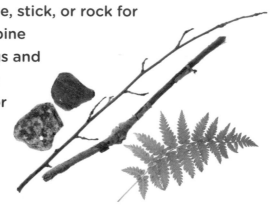

Here's a fun way to make art on the trail!

1 Think of a critter you want to make — a fierce bug, a big bird, or a friendly animal.

2 Look for a leaf, pinecone, stick, or rock for the body. Collect long pine needles or twigs for legs and whiskers. Pick up acorn caps and large seeds for eyes. Look for dried leaves or milkweed pods to make wings.

3 Arrange your nature finds on the ground. Put the eyes, legs, whiskers, wings, and tail on the critter's body.

Now give your critter a name and take a photo. Leave your critter where you created it!

This is Twiggy!

Toads

TOADS ARE AMPHIBIANS (am-FIB-ee-uns), which means they are usually born in the water but live much of their adult lives on land. Although they look like frogs, most toads have dry, warty skin, unlike a frog's smooth, moist skin. Toads are also chubbier than frogs and use their short legs to hop and crawl across the ground.

Eastern American toad

Amphibians are cold-blooded and depend on the sun to keep warm!

What kinds of **AMPHIBIANS** do you see?

Great Plains toad

Red-spotted toad

Western toad

Dwarf American toad

Listen for frog and toad calls. Now ribbit and croak back at them!

Leopard frog

Spring peeper

Wood frog

American bullfrog

Frogs and toads catch insects with their tongues and swallow their prey whole!

Tiger salamander

Red eft
(juvenile eastern newt)

Take a LOOK

Look for tadpoles in a pond in the spring. Catch a few in a jar and take a closer look.

ANiMAL HiDE & SEEK

Get moving with a predator-prey game!

Every animal needs to eat to stay alive. **PREDATORS** hunt other animals. **PREY** are the animals that predators eat.

TO PLAY THIS GAME, decide who wants to be the predator. Everyone else is the prey. You can be any animal you want — the predator tries to catch all the others. Here are some ideas!

PREDATOR		PREY	
Owl	Snake	Mosquito	Worm
Fox	Bear	Mice	Fish
Spider	Robin	Rabbit	Fly
Toad	Hawk	Moth	Squirrel

WHILE THE PREDATOR COUNTS TO TEN, the prey find hiding spot(s), such as behind a big rock, under a bush, or in the tall grass. Now the predator goes on the hunt! If the predator finds its prey, the prey may still be able to escape if they can run away fast enough! The first prey animal caught becomes the next predator.

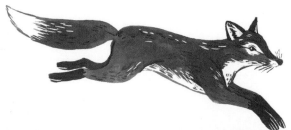

TOUCH IT!

Stop along the trail and use your hands to explore. Can you find and feel all these different textures?

Something
ROUGH

Something
WET

Something
SOFT

Something
WARM

Something
SMOOTH

Something
STICKY

Something
PRICKLY

Something
DRY

Something
COOL

Mushrooms

A MUSHROOM IS A TYPE OF FUNGUS. Unlike a plant, it doesn't need sunlight or seeds to grow. Many mushrooms grow near trees where they help recycle dead leaves and keep soil healthy.

WARNING: *Many mushrooms are poisonous. Never touch, pick, or eat a wild mushroom.*

Bonnet mushrooms

The mold you find on old bread is a type of fungus!

What kinds of **MUSHROOMS** do you see?

Coral fungus

Oyster

Chanterelle

Puffball

Morel

Look for mushrooms on stumps, on trees, and in grassy areas after a rainfall.

Turkey tail

Tinder fungus

Hair cap moss

What else do you see growing on or near trees?

Crusty lichen

Fern moss

Leafy lichen

Cushion moss

Take a LOOK

A mat of moss may look like one big, flat plant, but it's actually made up of lots of little plants bunched close together.

Nature
PAINT BRUSHES

If you like painting, you'll love making your own paint brushes! For this project, you'll need to bring along some string and a pair of scissors.

1 Find a few sturdy twigs for your brush handles. Collect a handful of evergreen needles, leaves, or flowers for your paint bristles.

2 Arrange the bristles around one end of your twig. While holding the bristles in place, wrap the string around them at the base of the brush. Wrap the string around several times and pull it tight, so the bristles will stay on the brush handle.

3 Knot your string, and trim off any long ends.

4 Test out your new nature brush by dipping it in a nearby stream or puddle and painting with water or mud on a rock.

Try painting the different animals and plants you've seen on your walk, or portraits of your fellow hikers.

PUT YOUR PATCH HERE

Seeds

ALL PLANTS GROW FROM SEEDS. Seeds come in many shapes and sizes. A seed can stay "asleep" for years until it finds a good spot with enough water and light to grow.

↑
Milkweed seed

Some plants, like milkweed, have pods that hold a bunch of seeds.

What kinds of **SEEDS** do you see?

Pinecone

An acorn's little cap is called a cupule.

Acorns (from an oak tree)

Pine seeds

Sweet gum

Horse chestnut

...then pooping them out!

Maple

Some seeds are spread by animals eating them, then pooping them out!

Lupine

Dandelion

How many seeds can you hold in one hand?

Take a LOOK

Tiny dandelion seeds use their fluff to catch the wind and sail like little parachutes to new land!

Nature
MANDALAS

A mandala is a circle with patterns in it that you can make almost anywhere out of nearly anything. All the supplies you need can be found on your walk!

1 To make your nature mandala, collect a bunch of leaves, flowers, pinecones, sticks, or stones. Next, find a smooth open surface on the ground.

2 Place some of your treasures on the ground to form the center of your mandala, then line up more objects to form larger circles and spokes surrounding the center.

3 Your nature mandala can be as big or small, and as simple or fancy, as you like! Try alternating different colors or shapes to create special patterns within your mandala.

You can take a photo of your mandala when you are finished, but part of the fun is leaving it in nature.

I SEE IT!

PUT YOUR PATCH HERE

Flowers

FLOWERS START OUT AS BUDS, THEN TURN INTO SEEDS, which is where new flowers come from. Many flowers have bright colors or strong smells to help attract pollinators.

When these insects and birds poke into flowers looking for nectar to eat, pollen sticks to their bodies or beaks. Then when they visit a new flower, some of that pollen rubs off inside and makes a seed.

Hepatica

Ants, flies, moths, and even mosquitoes spread pollen.

What kinds of **FLOWERS** do you see?

Dame's rocket

How many wildflowers can you smell?

Queen Anne's lace

Buttercup

Violet

Which flowers do bees and butterflies like best?

Daisy

Clover

Chicory

Daylily

Take a LOOK

Look closely inside a flower. That dusty yellow-orange stuff is the pollen.

FROM SEED TO FLOWER

Follow the pictures below to see how a seed grows into a flower.

A seed is watered by rain and begins to grow.

It feels warmth from the sun and sends roots down into the ground.

The plant stem shoots up above the earth's surface.

The stem grows tall and adds leaves and flowers.

SMELL IT!

You can experience nature with your sense of smell. Use your nose to sniff out these items, then fill in the checklist below.

- ☐ A flower
- ☐ A patch of mud
- ☐ Green grass
- ☐ Wet leaves

- ☐ Pine needles
- ☐ Tree sap
- ☐ Fungus or moss
- ☐ Something stinky

What else can you smell?

_____

_____

Butterflies

BUTTERFLIES ARE INSECTS THAT START OUT AS CRAWLY CATERPILLARS. Caterpillars munch lots of leaves until a hard case called a chrysalis (KRI-suh-lus) forms around their bodies. They stay hidden inside for a while, then emerge as butterflies!

Clouded sulphur butterfly

Butterflies taste with their feet!

Butterflies have bright, patterned wings. They sip flower nectar with their long tongues.

What kinds of **BUTTERFLIES** do you see?

A butterfly's wings are very delicate.

Swallowtail

Buckeye

Wood nymph

Painted lady

Monarch

Watch a butterfly to see where it lands!

Fritillary

Cabbage white

Red-spotted purple

Has a butterfly ever landed on you?

Take a LOOK

Check the underside of leaves to look for tiny butterfly eggs.

Nature
IMPRESSIONS

Create a memory of your walk with a nature impression!
Bring along some air-dry clay for this activity.

1 Look for acorns, seed pods, ferns, evergreen branches, leaves, or any other textured nature finds you'd like to press into clay.

2 Roll out and flatten a handful of clay.

3 Place your nature find on the clay's surface, and press the item down into the clay with your palm.

4 Pull the item away and look at the impression it left in the clay.

5 Back home, let your nature impressions dry for a few days in a safe place to make a permanent memory of your nature walk!

Objects with interesting textures or shapes make great designs.

Spiders

SPIDERS MAKE SILK IN THEIR BODIES AND WEAVE STICKY WEBS TO CATCH THEIR PREY. They wrap their eggs in silk and use strands of it to sail through the air from one place to another.

It takes most spiders about an hour to spin an elaborate web.

Orb web

When a spider feels its web shaking, it knows it caught a bug.

What kinds of **SPIDERS** do you see?

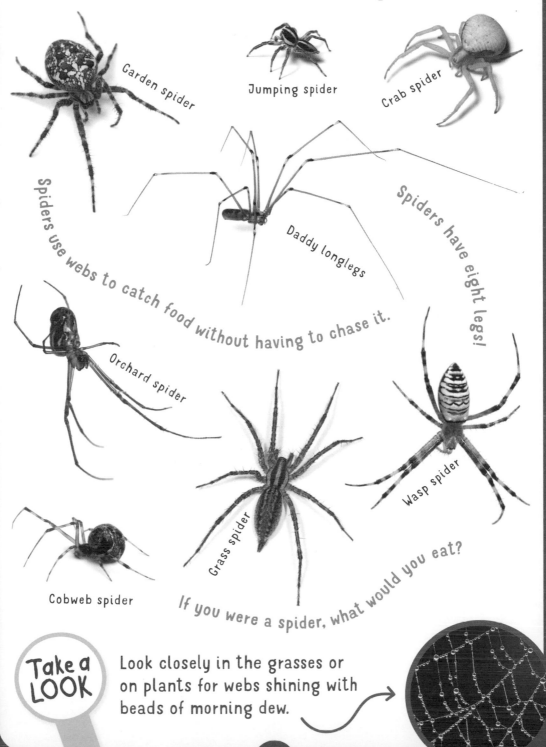

Garden spider

Jumping spider

Crab spider

Daddy longlegs

Spiders use webs to catch food without having to chase it.

Spiders have eight legs!

Orchard spider

Wasp spider

Grass spider

Cobweb spider

If you were a spider, what would you eat?

Take a LOOK

Look closely in the grasses or on plants for webs shining with beads of morning dew.

WHO EATS WHAT?

Wild animals have many different diets. **Carnivores**, such as wolves, eat only meat. **Herbivores**, such as deer, eat only plants. Some animals, like bears, are **omnivores** — they eat both plants and meat. Follow the colored line from each animal to see all the different things it eats. For example, find the fox in the blue circle and follow the matching blue line to learn that a fox eats squirrels, songbirds, mice, and berries.

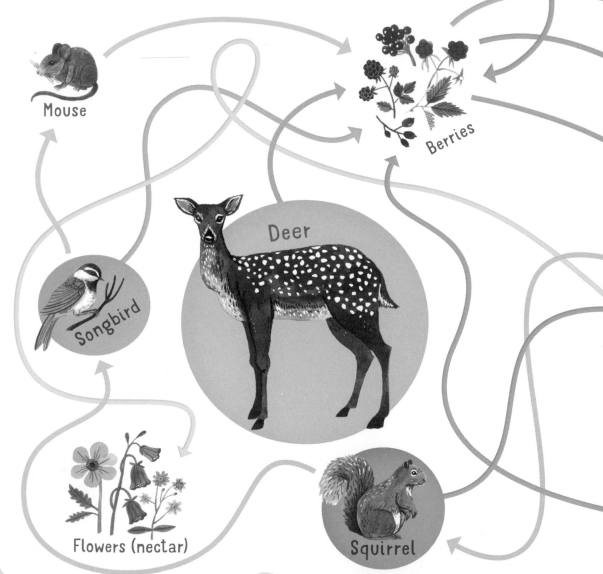

Mouse

Berries

Deer

Songbird

Flowers (nectar)

Squirrel

Tree buds

Fox

Insects

Bee

Bear

Seeds

Toad

Grasses

Fish

Tracks

ANIMALS LEAVE FOOTPRINTS BEHIND when they walk or run. A deer hoofprint looks very different from a tiny mouse track, a webbed duck print, or a dog track with claw marks.

Tracks can tell us what animals live nearby, what direction they are traveling, and if they are alone or in a group.

White-tailed deer hoofprint

The best place to find tracks is in mud, sand, or fresh snow.

What kinds of **TRACKS** do you see?

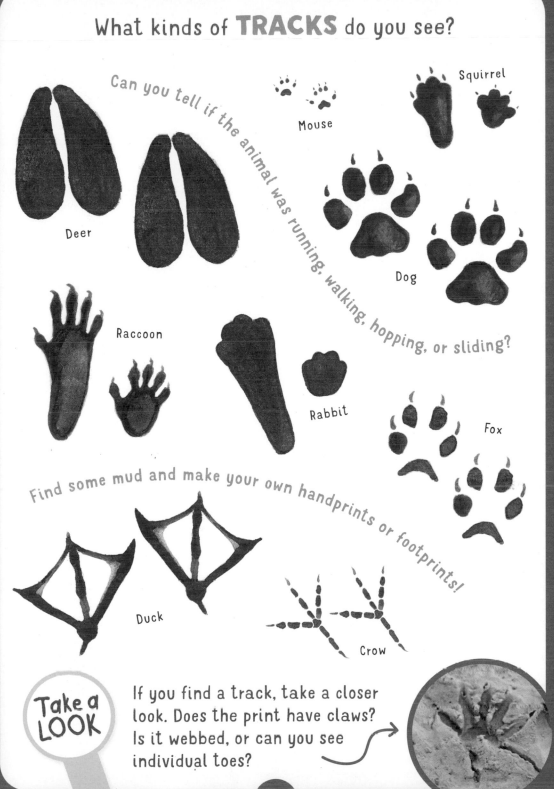

Can you tell if the animal was running, walking, hopping, or sliding?

Mouse

Squirrel

Deer

Dog

Raccoon

Rabbit

Fox

Find some mud and make your own handprints or footprints!

Duck

Crow

Take a LOOK

If you find a track, take a closer look. Does the print have claws? Is it webbed, or can you see individual toes?

MAKE A MAP
OF YOUR ADVENTURE

Use the foldout map and stickers on the following pages to record where you went, what you saw, and what the weather was like.

(**START**) your path at one side of the map and use the **arrows** ➡ to show which direction you walked. Along the way, put stickers of any landmarks you came across, such as a **fallen log** or a **big boulder**.

Did you see any **mountain peaks** or **creatures**? Did you pass any structures, like a **picnic table** or a **campfire ring**? Did you cross over a **bridge** or walk past a **pond**? And don't forget to mark the **END** of your path.

TRAIL MARKERS

Most trails have markers along the way so hikers don't get lost. These are usually paint marks or signs on trees. Sometimes stacks of rocks called **cairns** (KAYRNS) are used to guide the way. Did you see any markers on your walk?

The mission of Storey Publishing is to serve our customers by publishing practical information that encourages personal independence in harmony with the environment.

Text by Kathleen Yale
Edited by Deanna F. Cook and Lisa H. Hiley
Art direction and book design by Jessica Armstrong
Cover and interior illustrations by © Oana Befort,
  except page 47 by Jessica Armstrong
Photography by © Kimberly Stoney

Additional photography by © 4kodiak/iStock.com, 27 b.r.; © Aevenson/iStock.com, 47; © AlasdairJames/iStock.com, 19 centipede and earwig; © Aleksandar Stokic/Shutterstock, 27 turkey tail;   © Aleksey Suvorov/Dreamstime, 2; © Alexander Potapov/Dreamstime, 7 feather; © Alexandr Gryzlov/iStock.com, 20 pebbles; © AlexSava/iStock.com, 43 wasp spider; © Alius Imago/Shutterstock, ii, 14; © alto-cumulus/iStock.com, 35 chicory; © Ana Gram/Shutterstock, 7 crow; © Antagain/iStock.com, 25 row 2 l., 27 cushion moss & hair cap moss, 43 crab spider; © Anton-Burakov/Shutterstock, 27 crusty lichen; © Antonel/iStock.com, 35 clover; © badahos/Shutterstock, 19 larvae; © BigJoker/iStock.com, 28 t.; © Billion Photos/Shutterstock, 31 dandelion; © bonchan/iStock.com, 27 morel; © bonchan/Shutterstock, 35 violet; © Brian Guest/iStock.com, 12 b.r.; © Charles Brutlag/Dreamstime, 7 chickadee; © Charles Brutlag/Shutterstock, 7 cardinal; © chengyuzheng/iStock.com, 23 American bullfrog, 27 oyster mushroom; © Chris Mattison/Alamy Stock Photo, 23 Great Plains toad; © Christopher L. Nelson, 42; © Chutharat Kamkhuntee/Shutterstock, 25 row 2 r.; © Chutima Chaochaiya/Shutterstock, 5 & 25 row 1 l.; © Creative Imagery/iStock.com, 23 leopard frog; © CreativeNature_nl/iStock.com, 15 mouse; © ddggg/iStock.com, 26; © defun/iStock.com, 11 honeybee; © digi_guru/iStock.com, 12 l.; © Digitalimagined/Dreamstime, 19 woodlouse, 31 lupine; © dionisvero/iStock.com, 31 & 40 (acorns l.); © DirkRietschel/iStock.com, 35 buttercup; © Dobryanska Olga/Shutterstock, 35 daylily; © domnitsky/Shutterstock, 31 pine cone/seeds; © Elenarts/iStock.com, 38; © Elenathewise/iStock.com, 35 daisy; © Elliotte Rusty Harold/Shutterstock, 11 firefly; © epantha/iStock.com, 11 cricket; © Eric Isselee/Shutterstock, 43 cobweb spider; © fotogaby/iStock.com, 43 b.r.; © Franziska Krause/Dreamstime.com, 31 & 40 (acorns r.); © GA161076/iStock.com: 31 b.r.; © Gerald A. DeBoer/Shutterstock, 23 tiger salamander; © Gerald Deboer/Dreamstime.com, 23 spring

peeper; © GlobalP/iStock.com, 11 grasshopper, 15 chipmunk, 19 ant & snail, 43 garden spider; © groveb/iStock.com, 39 monarch; © guentermanaus/Shutterstock, 27 coral fungus; © Guy45/iStock.com, 11 fly; © Henrik_L/iStock.com, 11 mosquito; © hsvrs/iStock.com, 27 tinder fungus; © ian35mm/iStock.com, 23 tadpoles; © irin-k/Shutterstock, 11 beetle; © ivanastar/iStock.com, 20 sticks m.; © jacquesdurocher/iStock.com, 23 wood frog; © jat306/iStock.com: 12 t.r.; © J.K. York/Shutterstock, 43 orchard spider; Judy Gallagher/Wikimedia Commons, 34 grass spider; © Kaphoto/iStock.com, 11 ant; © kumeda/iStock.com, 25 row 1 c.; © KursanovV/iStock.com, 39 painted lady; © Labrador Photo Video/Shutterstock, 3 ash, aspen; © Le Thuy Do/Dreamstime, 3, 20, 32 (fern); © Iurii Kachkovskyi/Shutterstock, 39 cabbage white; © Iurii Konoval/Dreamstime, 3 nettle; © Manuel Liebeke, 18; © Maria Jeffs/Shutterstock, 15 baby rabbit; © mariedaloia/123RF, 7 sparrow; © Mark Follon/Alamy Stock Photo, 15 rabbit; © Matt Jeppson/Shutterstock, 23 red-spotted toad; © Matveev Aleksandr/iStock.com, 25 row 2 c.; © Melinda Fawver/Shutterstock, 23 red eft; © Mr. Rawin Tanpin/Shutterstock, 19 millipede; © Musat/iStock.com, 39 fritillary; © Nadezhda Nesterova/Shutterstock, 35 dame's rocket; © Nataliia_Melnychuk/iStock.com, 35 b.r.; © newannyart/iStock.com, 25 row 3 l.; © NNehring/iStock.com, 23 Western toad; © No Derog/iStock.com, 31 sweet gum; © Oleksandr Lytvynenko/Shutterstock, 7 duck; © Ovydyborets/Dreamstime, 3 horse chestnut & b.r.; © Paul Looyen/Shutterstock, 43 daddy long legs; © Pavel Krasensky/Shutterstock, 19 b.r.; © pengpeng/iStock.com, 43 jumping spider; © Peter Gudella/Shutterstock, 25 row 3 c.; © Rodmacivor/iStock.com, 30; © ronniechua/iStock.com, 7 robin; © Rosalba Matta-Machado/Shutterstock, 39 b.r.; © Samuel Brown/Dreamstime.com, 23 dwarf American toad; © Saso Novoselic, 34; © Scisetti Alfio/Shutterstock, 3 dandelion; © sirapob/iStock.com: 13 r.; © sittipong_srikanya/iStock.com, 1 background; © spline_x/Shutterstock, 27 leafy lichen; © Spondylolithesis/iStock.com, 7 hawk; © Steve Byland/iStock.com, 7 hummingbird; © Stevenrussellsmithphotos/Dreamstime, 3 maple & oak, 7 dove, 39 buckeye, red-spotted purple & swallowtail; © Stevenrussellsmithphotos/Shutterstock, 39 wood nymph; © stockphotofan11/Shutterstock, 15 b.r.; © suefeldberg/iStock.com, 15 squirrel; © Tathoms/Shutterstock, 7